TEEN GUIDE TO SOCIAL & EMOTIONAL SKILLS

DEVELOPING
SELF-MANAGEMENT

by Jennifer Kaul

BrightPoint Press

San Diego, CA

© 2023 BrightPoint Press
an imprint of ReferencePoint Press, Inc.
Printed in the United States

For more information, contact:
BrightPoint Press
PO Box 27779
San Diego, CA 92198
www.BrightPointPress.com

ALL RIGHTS RESERVED.

No part of this work covered by the copyright hereon may be reproduced or used in any form or by any means—graphic, electronic, or mechanical, including photocopying, recording, taping, web distribution, or information storage retrieval systems—without the written permission of the publisher.

LIBRARY OF CONGRESS CATALOGING-IN-PUBLICATION DATA

Names: Kaul, Jennifer, author.
Title: Developing self-management / by Jennifer Kaul.
Description: San Diego, CA : BrightPoint Press, [2023] | Series: Teen guide to social & emotional skills | Includes bibliographical references and index. | Audience: Grades 10-12
Identifiers: LCCN 2022001686 (print) | LCCN 2022001687 (eBook) | ISBN 9781678204402 (hardcover) | ISBN 9781678204419 (eBook)
Subjects: LCSH: Self-management (Psychology)--Juvenile literature. | Stress management-- Juvenile literature.
Classification: LCC BF632 .K38 2023 (print) | LCC BF632 (eBook) | DDC 158.1--dc23/ eng/20220119
LC record available at https://lccn.loc.gov/2022001686
LC eBook record available at https://lccn.loc.gov/2022001687

CONTENTS

AT A GLANCE   4

INTRODUCTION   6
    WHAT IS SELF-MANAGEMENT?

CHAPTER ONE   14
    SELF-MANAGEMENT AT SCHOOL

CHAPTER TWO   32
    SELF-MANAGEMENT AT HOME

CHAPTER THREE   48
    SELF-MANAGEMENT WITH FRIENDS

CHAPTER FOUR   62
    SELF-MANAGEMENT IN THE COMMUNITY

Glossary   74
Source Notes   75
For Further Research   76
Index   78
Image Credits   79
About the Author   80

AT A GLANCE

- Self-management relates to managing emotions and reactions to live a happy and healthy life.

- Setting goals, making plans, staying organized, reducing stress, and advocating for oneself are important self-management skills.

- There are ways to build and use self-management skills at school, at home, with friends, and in the community.

- Self-management skills are an important part of a being a good student. Working well with others and staying on top of assignments can help teens succeed in school.

- Self-management skills can also be used at home. Setting personal goals and planning to achieve them can make life more enjoyable and offer people a sense of accomplishment.

- Interactions with friends can also benefit from the use of self-management skills. Self-management can help teens maintain positive relationships with friends while also making their own decisions.

- People's communities can benefit from their use of self-management skills. Managing stress and taking initiative can help people maximize their time and efforts in making the world a better place.

- Self-management skills are an important part of a balanced life, regardless of the setting.

INTRODUCTION

WHAT IS SELF-MANAGEMENT?

Ben walked through the halls of his high school on his way to algebra class. As he neared the door, he stopped in his tracks. *Oh no*, he thought, dragging a hand through his hair. He'd forgotten to do his homework.

What am I going to do? he wondered. Ms. Jackson was strict. And since he

Developing self-management skills can be helpful in a school setting.

typically turned in his assignments on time, he didn't know how she'd react.

Ben took a few deep breaths to calm himself. Then he considered his options.

He didn't have time to do the assignment now. He could lie and say he'd submitted it and it must've been deleted somehow. He could deal with getting a lower grade. Or, he could tell her the truth and ask for an extension. After a moment of hesitation, Ben knew what he had to do.

Ben entered the classroom and slowly made his way to Ms. Jackson's desk.

"Hi, Ms. Jackson," he said.

She smiled at him. "Hello, Ben."

"I forgot to do my assignment. Is there any way I could turn it in later today?"

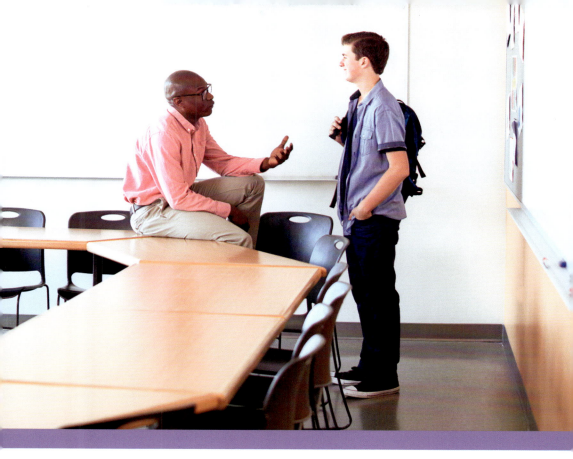

Sometimes, being truthful and asking for help can be a simple solution to a student's problem.

She thought for a moment, her smile becoming thinner. Finally, she nodded. "Everyone forgets things from time to time. The important thing is how you react when it happens. If you send me the assignment before class tomorrow, I'll give you full credit."

Ben felt the tension in his body begin to fade. "Thanks, Ms. Jackson."

"Thank yourself," she told him. "I'll look forward to receiving your assignment."

As soon as he was in his seat, Ben took out his tablet and added the assignment to his planner. The last thing he wanted was to forget about it again.

SELF-MANAGEMENT

Social and emotional learning, or SEL, is an important part of a happy,

Writing down notes on a tablet or notebook can help people be organized and manage their time wisely.

healthy life. The areas involved in SEL are self-awareness, self-management, social awareness, relationship skills, and responsible decision-making skills. Each area can be broken down into smaller subsets of skills.

The Collaborative for Academic, Social, and Emotional Learning, or CASEL for short, defines self-management as "the abilities to manage one's emotions, thoughts, and behaviors effectively in different situations and to achieve goals and aspirations."[1] It includes skills and strategies related to managing stress and other emotions, acting with **self-discipline** and self-motivation, and setting goals. It also covers making plans, staying organized, taking **initiative**, and having **agency**.

Self-management skills can be learned, practiced, and developed. Developing

Self-management skills can help increase personal growth and overall happiness.

self-management skills can help people in all aspects of life. This includes being happy and successful at school, at home, with friends, and in the community.

CHAPTER ONE

SELF-MANAGEMENT AT SCHOOL

One day, in biology class, Ben sat with a group of his classmates. They had just been assigned a group project on endangered species but were struggling to figure out how to get started. Ben listened intently as his groupmates shared their thoughts.

Having clear communication can help group projects succeed.

"There are so many angles we could take," Bailey said. "A specific endangered species, or maybe a human activity that harms animal species. Unfortunately, there are a lot of options to choose from for both."

"What about how people can help endangered species?" Mika asked as Rena nodded in agreement. "There are lots of groups that work to protect animals and their habitats. That's important too."

They were all silent for a moment, lost in thought. Ben had an idea, but he wasn't sure if he should share it. What if the others didn't like it? Maybe it would be better to let them make the decision. But as he waited for someone else to speak up, Ben

Sharing ideas with a large group can be scary.

realized he liked his idea. Maybe the others would too.

"Those are some really good ideas," he began. "What if we combine them all?"

The others watched him, listening carefully. Ben began to feel more confident as he spoke. "We could create a presentation that features different endangered species," Ben continued. "It could include how endangered the species is and what's causing the decrease in its population. The last few slides can show what people can do to help, and anything else we want to add."

The others slowly nodded. "That's a good idea," Rena said. Mika smiled, and Bailey gave Ben a thumbs-up.

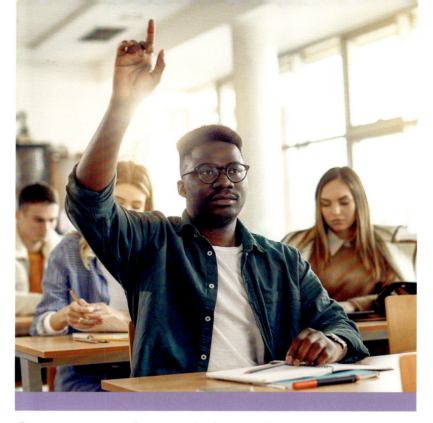

Courage can play a role in small, everyday actions.

Ben felt proud of himself for sharing his thoughts and getting the group started. He took a moment to appreciate this feeling. Then, he and his groupmates began to plan out their project together.

COURAGE TO TAKE INITIATIVE

Ben took initiative when he shared his ideas with his group. This not only helped his group, but it also made Ben feel capable and proud. Still, taking initiative isn't always easy.

Taking initiative involves courage. Many people think of courage as being brave in the face of danger. However, courage can take many forms.

Courage involves pushing past what feels comfortable and easy. It can mean being open and honest about how someone is

Self-management can mean taking steps to practice courage. For example, being part of a team sport can involve courage.

feeling. It can mean standing up for what is right. These things take courage.

To develop courage, a person can notice how the people in her life model it. She can read books about characters who do the same. It can help to see how others handle similar problems and how they develop positive traits.

Having courage comes with many benefits. According to educational psychologist Michele Borba, "Courage . . . boosts kids' resilience, confidence, and willpower as well as their learning, performance and school engagement."[2]

Once people have the courage to take initiative, they can take small steps. They can speak up when they have a question or an idea to share. It can start with a small group of people they trust. Later, they can try sharing their thoughts with a larger group such as the whole class. They can also try new hobbies or activities, like learning to play an instrument or trying out for a sports team.

TIPS FOR BUILDING CONFIDENCE

There are many steps people can take to gain confidence. First, they can watch their body language. Sitting straight and making eye contact can help. Getting enough sleep and exercise can also boost a person's mood and self-esteem. Another way people can gain confidence is by being positive. They can think and speak positively about themselves and be willing to accept praise. They can recite affirmations, or positive sayings, about themselves and their ability to achieve.

It can be worth taking initiative, even when it feels like a challenge. The more practice someone gets with taking initiative, the easier it will become. However, when trying new things, it is important to make sure decisions are safe and smart.

COLLECTIVE GOAL-SETTING

Ben worked with his group to make decisions about their project. It can be a challenge to set goals as a group, but it can also be gratifying. This goes beyond the success of a single project. According to businessman Josh Steimle, "Developing the right habits when it comes to working with

Assigning roles to each person can help a group work more efficiently.

others will result in leadership opportunities, higher pay, and more rewarding work."[3]

When goal-setting with a group at school, it is important that everyone's ideas are heard. It can help to assign group roles.

These help everyone feel involved and keep the group on track. Roles can include a leader, a timekeeper, a recorder, and more.

Group members can start goal-setting by sharing their ideas. They can then work together to choose the idea that would work

WORKING WELL WITH OTHERS

There are many things people can do to help a group succeed. They can listen when other group members speak. They can keep an open mind and give others credit for the work they do. In addition, they can stay positive about the project and their groupmates. They can compromise when needed. They can do their part and take responsibility if they make a mistake.

best. If there is a disagreement, the group can vote to make the final decision.

PLANNING AND ORGANIZING

After discussing their project, Ben's group started planning and organizing tasks. This is especially important when several people are involved. The project's success depends on the group working together. Everyone must have a clear understanding of the group's goals and deadlines. They must know their individual responsibilities too.

A group's first step can be to list the tasks they must complete. They can then

Organizing ideas on sticky notes or in a notebook can help keep a group on track.

decide the order in which these should be done and how long each task should take. These tasks can then be split up among group members.

It is helpful if the group can set checkpoints. They can use set dates to check in with each other and note progress. This helps the project stay on track.

There are many instances beyond group work in which teamwork is important. Extracurricular clubs, sports, and activities often involve working together. This can help participants learn, have fun, and achieve. For example, students in a school play rely on each other to learn their lines and show up for performances.

Groups of friends also depend on each other in school. It can be comforting and

Self-management can look like investing in friendships at school.

fun to catch up with friends between classes or at lunch. Friends can discuss information shared in class. They can share the day's highs and lows. This can help make school more enjoyable.

Self-management is an important part of a school career. It can help people achieve academic success and navigate social interactions. It can also allow them to make the most of extracurricular activities.

CHAPTER TWO

SELF-MANAGEMENT AT HOME

Ben arrived home from school and checked his phone. A notification popped up, telling him his friend had invited him to play an online video game. It was one of his best friends and one of his favorite games. Ben started to open the game on his phone. Then he stopped and glanced at his backpack. He had

Playing video games all day is not good time management when there are many tasks to finish.

homework and an upcoming test he

needed to study for.

Ben didn't know what to do. He really

wanted to play the game. He would

probably have enough time to do his

Having a planner or calendar helps remind people of the things they need to do.

homework later. Still, one of Ben's goals was to do well in school. He didn't want to risk getting a lower grade than he was capable of earning. He decided to check his planner to make sure he didn't have anything else going on that night.

When Ben opened his planner on his phone, he saw he had basketball practice later that evening. He was disappointed, but he knew what he had to do. He sent his friend a text saying he had too much going on that night. His friend responded that he understood and they'd have to play some other time soon. Ben tucked his phone into his pocket, took out his homework, and got to work.

The next day, Ben didn't have much homework. Once he finished it up, he

Good time management lets people have less stress and more fun.

sent his friend a game request. His friend accepted. Ben enjoyed playing the game without worrying about falling behind on anything else.

SELF-DISCIPLINE AND SELF-MOTIVATION

Ben showed self-discipline when he chose to do his homework instead of playing the video game with his friend. This helped him finish what he needed to get done. Self-discipline involves taking control of oneself. It allows people to do what they know is right instead of giving in to what sounds fun in the moment.

There are many ways to build self-discipline. One way is to create good habits and routines. A good habit could involve checking a planner after arriving home. It could mean having time set aside

Creating good habits, like washing the dishes right after using them, can build self-discipline.

for homework. Turning off or silencing smartphones and other devices can help people stay focused. Having a regular sleep schedule can help improve mood, focus, and overall health.

INDIVIDUAL GOAL-SETTING

Ben decided to check his planner because of his goal of doing well in school. Having goals helps people motivate themselves to do the things they want in life. People can

SMART GOALS

It is helpful to make SMART goals. Peter Drucker created the idea of SMART goals in 1954. SMART is an acronym for: S—specific, M—measurable, A—achievable, R—realistic, T—time-based. When someone sets a specific goal, she knows exactly what she's trying to achieve. A measurable goal can be tracked for progress and completion. An achievable goal is one that is realistic for the person to meet. A realistic goal makes sense with what the person hopes to accomplish. A time-based goal has a deadline.

make goals for almost anything they wish to accomplish. This can include doing well in school, saving money, being healthier, or getting better at something they love.

It can help to break large goals into smaller parts. This can make the goal feel more manageable. It can also help to write down the goal, think about challenges in reaching it, and track progress.

PLANNING AND ORGANIZING

People cannot remember everything. For example, Ben forgot he had basketball practice until he checked his planner. He may have chosen to play the game had

Some people use bullet journals to help them keep track of habits, important tasks, and even their moods.

he not checked his schedule. Then he might not have gotten his homework done on time. Staying organized and planning ahead helps people meet their goals.

Having a planner and a to-do list can help people plan ahead. Planning ahead means making sure there is enough time to do the tasks that need to get done. It is important to think about upcoming

> ### URGENT VS. IMPORTANT MATRIX
>
> The **Urgent** vs. Important Matrix can help people order tasks. When a task is urgent, it must be done soon. When a task is important, it holds great value. Some tasks are both urgent and important, some are one or the other, and some are neither. This can help people decide which tasks need to be done right away. It can also help them see which tasks they need to plan for and which might not need to be done at all.

events and activities to plan around them. People can also prioritize tasks, figuring out the order in which they should be done.

In addition to organizing tasks, people can organize their materials. Many people do this by subject or by item type. For example, students often use folders to organize their files. They might have a folder for each class with subfolders for different projects and assignments. They might organize their email in a similar fashion. They could have emails from family and friends in one folder and school-related messages in another. This helps their inbox stay organized. It also makes it easier to find things.

The same can be done with physical papers using binders, folders, and notebooks. It is important to regularly review papers and files. People can then remove unneeded materials to make sure everything stays organized.

Having an organized space can help people succeed. This means having an area for work that is free of clutter and other distractions. A clean space makes it easier to gather needed materials and stay focused. A health care system called

An organized and clean space can help with focus and with getting a good night's sleep.

Nemours Children's Health suggests, "If you need more tips on staying focused, ask a teacher, school counselor, or a parent for help."[4]

An organized space is not only good for keeping track of school supplies. It can also help people create a relaxing and enjoyable place to spend their time. Getting organized means figuring out a good place for everything. This makes it easier to keep a room clean, which can save time and cut down on arguments with parents. This leaves the person with more time to focus on the things he enjoys.

Reducing clutter can also help. People can focus on the things they value and the things they need. They can then simplify by donating the rest. This can help them clear their spaces and calm their minds. Keeping a space clutter-free is also important to people's health. Dr. Jennifer

A messy room can negatively impact a person's mental health.

Verdolin wrote an article for *Psychology Today*. She says, "Keeping trash around, failing to clean regularly, or simply leaving your home in disarray can be a breeding ground for bacteria and potential diseases."[5] Using self-management at home can lead to both positive habits and a healthy mind and body.

CHAPTER THREE

SELF-MANAGEMENT WITH FRIENDS

Ben read the latest message in the group text with his friends. They were planning to go to an outdoor concert later that month. Ben wanted to go, but he was scheduled to work that same night.

He told his friends the problem. One friend sent a sad face emoji. Another said they'd all have to get together some other

Sometimes practicing self-management with friends can be difficult.

time. The third friend suggested he call in sick and skip his shift.

Ben stopped to think about his friend's idea. He really wanted to go to the concert with his friends. Still, he didn't want to lie

Journaling feelings can help organize conflicting emotions.

to his boss. He told his friends he'd think about it. Most of them were understanding, but a few kept bugging him about skipping work. Finally, Ben tossed his phone onto the couch, frustrated. He was trying to do the right thing. It felt like some of his friends couldn't understand that.

    He sat there for a few moments, then took out a notebook and a pen. He journaled about how upset he was with some of his friends and about how torn he felt. Once he'd gotten his feelings down on paper, he felt a bit better. He began a list of different ways to handle the situation. Then he got an idea. Maybe he could ask a coworker to switch shifts.

    Ben called his work and spoke with the manager. She was happy to ask if someone would be willing to switch shifts.

Minutes later, Ben texted his friends. He told them to go ahead and order tickets, including one for him.

MANAGING EMOTIONS

Ben felt upset when some of his friends pushed him to skip his shift at work. However, instead of pushing back or giving in, he managed his emotions. This gave him a chance to calm down and think more clearly. He accepted his feelings and knew he could choose how to react.

There are many ways to manage emotions. Some of these are healthy and others are not. Pushing negative emotions

Ignoring emotions can cause stress to the body.

away or ignoring emotions can cause the problem to build. Instead, it is best for people to work through their feelings and try to solve their problems. This might involve talking through the problem with a trusted family member or friend. It can also mean journaling or finding other ways to relax and reflect.

MEDITATION

Meditation is one way to manage emotions. It means focusing on the present moment, often by paying attention to the breath. Psychologist Dr. Tara Brach suggests a concept called RAIN:

First you recognize what is arising inside, then secondly set an intention to accept whatever it is, thirdly investigate it with interest and care, and lastly, nurture it with self-compassion.

Meditation has been proven to improve both mental and physical health.

Quoted in Jason N. Linder, "How Mindfulness Can Help Us Better Manage Our Emotions," Psychology Today, *April 13, 2019. www.psychologytoday.com.*

PERSONAL AGENCY

Ben stood his ground even when his friends wanted him to do otherwise. When he did this, he showed personal agency. Personal agency is making decisions for oneself instead of following along with what others want.

People can build their agency in many ways. First, they can spend time with people who make them feel good about themselves and their decisions. They can limit mindless actions such as scrolling through social media. Instead, they can use that time to learn something new, exercise, or enjoy time in nature.

When it is time to make a decision, people can use their agency by thinking things through. This might involve making a list of ideas. It can also mean talking things through with a trusted family member or friend. However, it is important not to become too dependent on others when making decisions. Building self-esteem and confidence can help people gain and make use of personal agency.

PERSONAL AGENCY & SOCIAL MEDIA

FEELINGS ABOUT SOCIAL MEDIA

Feel more connected to friends	81%
Feel able to show creative side	71%
Feel supported	68%
Feel overwhelmed by drama	45%
Feel pressure to post things that appeal to others	43%
Feel worse about themselves	26%

Source: Monica Anderson and Jingjing Jiang, "Teens and Their Experiences on Social Media," Pew Research Center, November 28, 2018. www.pewresearch.org.

In 2018, Pew Research Center surveyed teens to better understand their feelings about social media. While most teens surveyed felt social media had a positive effect on them in some way, many also found it harmed their agency and self-esteem.

TAKING INITIATIVE

Ben could have gone to work and missed out on a fun night with his friends. Instead, he chose to **advocate** for himself by calling his manager and asking to switch shifts. When people advocate for themselves, they share what they want and need. Advocating for oneself can mean asking for help. It can also take the form of sharing successes, preferences, or feelings.

Sometimes it is hard to take initiative with friends. People might worry about upsetting their friends or being seen as different. Still, true friends value each other for who

Teens can process feelings with a mentor or therapist, which can be a way of advocating for themselves.

A WIN-WIN ATTITUDE

When making a decision, it is best to find a solution that works well for everyone. Dr. Stephen R. Covey calls this a "Win-Win." According to franklincovey.com, someone with a win-win attitude has:

1. Integrity: sticking with your true feelings, values, and commitments; 2. Maturity: expressing your ideas and feelings with courage and consideration for the ideas and feelings of others; 3. Abundance Mentality: believing there is plenty for everyone.

By using these characteristics, people can ensure everyone is happy with the end result. This gets a person what she wants while also making her enjoyable to work with.

Quoted in "Habit 4: Think Win-Win," Franklin Covey, n.d. www.franklincovey.com.

they are. It is important for people to feel confident and comfortable with their friends. This encourages them to take initiative and to share their true thoughts and feelings.

While taking initiative involves making suggestions and taking action, it should be done in a positive way, so friends feel empowered. It should involve making positive changes rather than pressuring others into doing things that could be harmful. Self-management with friends is an important way to be true to oneself and to do what is right.

CHAPTER FOUR

SELF-MANAGEMENT IN THE COMMUNITY

Ben headed to the elementary school down the street. He smiled as he caught sight of the turning Ferris wheel and heard the gleeful screams of kids. After checking in with the school carnival's coordinator, he went to the ring toss game he would run that afternoon.

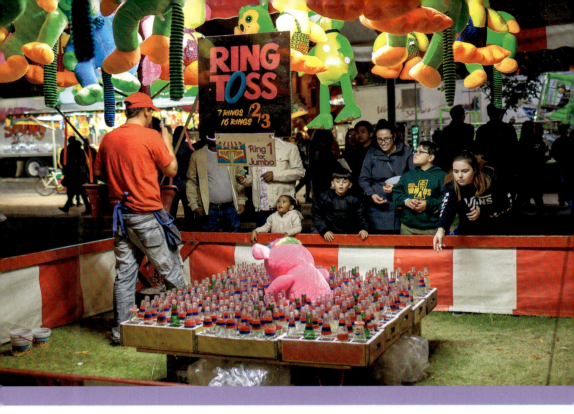

Working or volunteering in the community requires self-management skills.

"Hello!" Ben greeted a woman and her son as they approached. "Step right up and try your luck at the ring toss game!" The young boy happily handed Ben a ticket. He took the rings from Ben and tossed them toward the pegs, one at a time. Ben watched, impressed, as the boy got one, two, three, four of the five targets. If the boy got the last one, he'd win one of the large stuffed gorillas most kids had been eying since the carnival began.

The boy wound up and tossed the ring. It bounced off its target, then onto the pavement. "No!" the boy shouted, looking visibly upset.

"Great job!" his mother exclaimed. "You won!" She trained her gaze on Ben. "He wins the gorilla, right?"

Self-control and good communication are important skills to have when dealing with customers in a carnival or any other workplace.

Ben didn't know what to do. "I'm not sure," he said as more families lined up to play. "Let me ask." The woman began grumbling to a nearby parent as Ben looked for the coordinator. Soon, the woman began pestering him to just give her son the toy.

"My daughter's ring bounced off her third peg last night, and she didn't get credit for it," another parent complained. Ben finally found the supervisor. She calmly explained to the mother and her son that he had earned the four-peg prize. Once they had left, the coordinator congratulated Ben on a job well done.

STRESS MANAGEMENT

Ben felt stressed when the woman pushed him to do something he was unsure about. Still, he didn't let his stress control him.

Learning to manage stress is important to a person's mental and emotional health.

He remained calm. This helped him handle the situation.

People are faced with many stressful situations in life. According to the Mayo Clinic, "Your brain comes hard-wired with an alarm system for your protection. . . .

Unfortunately, the nonstop complications of modern life mean that some people's alarm systems rarely shut off."[6] People might feel stress when they forget to do something important. They might feel stress when they argue with someone they love. Learning how to manage this stress can help make such moments easier to get through.

Stress can trigger a physical reaction. This could be sweaty palms, a tense stomach, or a pounding heart. While stress can help people recognize danger, too much of it is unhealthy. Luckily, there are many ways to manage stress. Eating healthful foods, exercising, and getting enough sleep can decrease stress. There are also many techniques people can learn to manage stress. If people practice these

STRESS MANAGEMENT STRATEGIES

There are many ways to manage stress. Focused breathing can help people calm down. Scanning the body and noting areas of tension can help the body relax. People can also speak positively about themselves and picture things going well. This can help them gain confidence about the future. People can also spend time in nature, listen to music, talk with loved ones, or do something they enjoy.

strategies each day, they are more likely to be able to apply them when needed.

COLLECTIVE AGENCY

Ben may have wanted to give the boy the gorilla after the ring toss game. However, he knew he was part of something bigger. Many kids likely had their ring bounce off the target. It would be unfair for some of them to get credit while others did not.

Collective agency involves working with others. It means seeing how one's actions affect the entire group. The things people do in their communities can help or harm others. According to Gary Hopkins,

Interacting with different types of people within the community can help develop compassion and respect.

Education World's editor in chief, there are "five themes of **citizenship**—honesty, compassion, respect, responsibility, and courage."[7]

While every community is unique, the thing they have in common is the need for good citizens. Good citizens help their neighbors and take care of their neighborhood. They learn about what happens in their communities and participate in community events. Developing the themes of citizenship can

CIRCLE OF CONCERN

According to Dr. Stephen R. Covey, everyone has a Circle of Concern. This includes everything they're interested in, involved in, or worried about. However, it is impossible for people to do or solve things they don't have control over. To be effective, one can focus on his Circle of Influence. This is a smaller set of things within a person's Circle of Concern that the person can control.

help people better appreciate and support their communities.

SELF-MANAGEMENT AS A PART OF LIFE

Self-management skills can help people in many ways. Managing stress and other emotions can keep people happy and healthy. Meeting goals can help people find fulfillment. Having agency can help people take charge of their lives.

Self-management is just one of many skills involved in social and emotional learning. Many of these skills and areas support each other. By developing these skills, people can live happy, balanced lives.

GLOSSARY

advocate

to speak to one's needs or interests

agency

the ability to take control of oneself

citizenship

qualities that make someone a positive member of a community

initiative

the ability to ask questions or decide what to do without direction

meditation

the act of being calm and present or of deeply reflecting on life

self-discipline

the ability to take control of emotions and actions in order to pursue specific goals

urgent

needing to be done or taken care of right away

SOURCE NOTES

INDRODUCTION: WHAT IS SELF-MANAGEMENT?

1. "What Is the CASEL Framework?" *CASEL*, n.d. https://casel.org.

CHAPTER ONE: SELF-MANAGEMENT AT SCHOOL

2. Michele Borba, "9 Ways to Cultivate Courage in Kids," *U.S. News & World Report*, May 11, 2017. https://health.usnews.com.

3. Josh Steimle, "30 Simple Habits to Help You Work Well with Others," *Forbes*, February 18, 2015. www.forbes.com.

CHAPTER TWO: SELF-MANAGEMENT AT HOME

4. "Organizing Schoolwork & Assignments," *Nemours TeensHealth*, 2017. https://kidshealth.org.

5. Jennifer Verdolin, "Why Being Organized Matters," *Psychology Today*, August 4, 2019. www.psychologytoday.com

CHAPTER FOUR: SELF-MANAGEMENT IN THE COMMUNITY

6. Mayo Clinic Staff, "Stress Management," *Mayo Foundation for Medical Education and Research*, February 26, 2021. www.mayoclinic.org.

7. Gary Hopkins, "Teaching Good Citizenship's Five Themes," *Education World*, September 18, 2017. www.educationworld.com.

FOR FURTHER RESEARCH

BOOKS

Karen Bluth, PhD, *The Self-Compassionate Teen: Mindfulness and Compassion Skills to Conquer Your Critical Inner Voice*. Oakland, CA: New Harbinger Publications, 2020.

Kris Hirschmann, *Understanding Motivation*. San Diego, CA: ReferencePoint Press, 2018.

Barbara Sheen, *Teen Guide to Managing Stress and Anxiety*. San Diego, CA: ReferencePoint Press, 2022.

INTERNET SOURCES

Julie Corliss, "Six Relaxation Techniques to Reduce Stress," *Harvard Health Publishing*, September 10, 2019. www.health.harvard.edu.

"Emotional Intelligence," *Nemours TeensHealth*, n.d. https://kidshealth.org.

Mind Tools Content Team, "Personal Goal Setting: Planning to Live Your Life Your Way," *Mind Tools*, n.d. www.mindtools.com.

WEBSITES

Assets Coming Together (ACT) for Youth Center for Community Action
www.actforyouth.net

ACT for Youth is an initiative that works to promote positive youth development.

Collaborative for Academic, Social, and Emotional Learning (CASEL)
https://casel.org

CASEL is an organization that promotes social and emotional learning in schools.

Greater Good Science Center (GGSC)
https://ggie.berkeley.edu

The Greater Good Science Center studies and teaches skills to help improve society.

INDEX

Borba, Michele, 22
Brach, Tara, 54

carnivals, 62–66
CASEL, 12
Circle of Concern, 72
collective agency, 70
courage, 20–22, 60, 71
Covey, Stephen, 60, 72

Drucker, Peter, 39

goal-setting, 24–26, 39–40
group projects, 14–19, 24–29

Hopkins, Gary, 70–71

initiative, 12, 20, 22–24, 58–61

journaling, 51, 54

Mayo Clinic, 67
meditation, 54

Nemours Children's Health, 45

organized space, 44–47

personal agency, 55–56, 57
Pew Research Center, 57
planners, 10, 35, 37, 39, 40, 42

self-discipline, 12, 37–38
self-esteem, 23, 56, 57
social media, 55, 57
Steimle, Josh, 24–25
stress, 12, 66–69, 73

Verdolin, Jennifer, 46–47
video games, 32–33, 36, 37, 40

IMAGE CREDITS

Cover: © Dmytro Buianskyi/
iStockphoto
5: © Sengchoy Int/
Shutterstock Images
7: © Monkey Business Images/
Shutterstock Images
9: © Monkey Business Images/
Shutterstock Images
11: © Kali 9/iStockphoto
13: © Bear Fotos/Shutterstock Images
15: © Fat Camera/iStockphoto
17: © Monkey Business Images/
Shutterstock Images
19: © Drazen Zigic/
Shutterstock Images
21: © Monkey Business Images/
Shutterstock Images
25: © Seventy-Four/
Shutterstock Images
28: © Press Master/
Shutterstock Images
30: © Monkey Business Images/
Shutterstock Images
33: © Gorodenkoff/
Shutterstock Images

34: © Pra Chid/Shutterstock Images
36: © Aslysun/Shutterstock Images
38: © Dean Drobot/
Shutterstock Images
41: © Diana Parkhouse/
Shutterstock Images
45: © Seventy-Four/
Shutterstock Images
47: © Trek and Shoot/
Shutterstock Images
49: © Marian Fil/Shutterstock Images
50: © Alena Ozerova/
Shutterstock Images
53: © Fizkes/Shutterstock Images
57: © Red Line Editorial
59: © Digital Skillet/
Shutterstock Images
63: © Salvador Maniquiz/
Shutterstock Images
65: © Aaron Hawkins/iStockphoto
67: © Obradovic/iStockphoto
71: © DGL Images/iStockphoto

ABOUT THE AUTHOR

Jennifer Kaul is an author of children's and young adult literature who hopes to enccurage thought, spark conversation, and make the world a better place.